"Attacked by Wolves"

by
Ralph "Little Eagle" Williston

copyrite 2020
Little Eagle Publishing Co.
Dearborn, MO

Illustration by Joan Shaw

This book was edited by Nancy "Straight Arrow" Wiltse/Williston (Chippewa/Ojibwa)

ISBN 978-0-9707904-9-1

b

Table of Contents:

Chapter 1…………..Trapped in a Tree story……………………..p.1

Chapter 2……Stay Over Night In The Desert……………….p.5

Chapter 3……………..Finding Shelter……………………………….. p.11

Chapter Four…. Keeping the Wolves Out……………….p.15
  Falling Eagle story…………………………………………..p.16

Chapter Five ….,,Fast Turtle story…………………………….p.23

Chapter Six…Don't Speak With A Forked Tongue story….p.29

Chapter Seven…Follow The River story……………………….p.37

Chapter Eight… Beautiful Valley story…………………………..p.45

Chapter nine…..Healer With Blue Eyes story…………………p.49

Chapter ten…."From Your Author"……………………………….p.53
-Mini Table of Contents-
  The Perfect Man story……………………………….p. 54
  When I took our family to visit the Navajo……….p. 57
  The Pointing pole, a Choctaw Migration story…….p.60
  A town called Tahoka……………………………………..p.62
  A few things that I recall……………………………….p. 64
  Intro. to the "My White Dove" …………………..p. 65
  Intro. to "Run Over by Buffalo"……………………….p. 71
  Intro. To "Caught in a Flash Flood"……………….p. 75
  Intro. To "White Dove Catch Your Pony"…………..p.76
  Intro. To future Stories…………………………………..p.81
  End notes and pictures……………………………….p. 82

c

Illustration by Sheila Williston

(...Little Eagle is day dreaming as Grandfather tells stories and sees the picture above in his mind.)

d

Attacked by wolves
Chapter One
Trapped In A Tree

  While Grandfather was telling one of his stories, Little Eagle day dreamed as he was looking into the evening fire. Little Eagle remembered that Grandfather would always put his listeners into the story by saying, "If you...hunted all day and found nothing, and then you heard a sound way up in a tree. You thought, it must be a squirrel and squirrels are good to eat. So you climbed up into that tree and looked for squirrels in their nest, only to discover that the sound was made by two limbs rubbing across each other when the wind blew.

While you were hanging by your arms in that tree, a sudden wind blew really hard and you are now trying to find something to put your feet on so you would not fall.

You found a nice sturdy place to put one of your feet and was able to keep from falling. But when the strong wind stopped you felt something close in together, like a tight clamp, on your foot.

You looked down and you had put your foot right between the limbs that were rubbing together. The limbs had opened up and now the limbs had clamped tightly around your foot. You pulled up hard on your foot by pulling up by some limbs overhead to try to pull it out and it only hurt more.

You could not pull your foot out. You had lost your hatchet when the strong wind blew so you could not cut the limbs. You were able to balance yourself in that tree with the other foot and held on with your arms on some other limbs. You were too far from your village for anyone to hear your calls. You are now "Trapped In A Tree."

All night you tried to pull your foot out but it only hurt more.

Illustration by Straight Arrow Williston

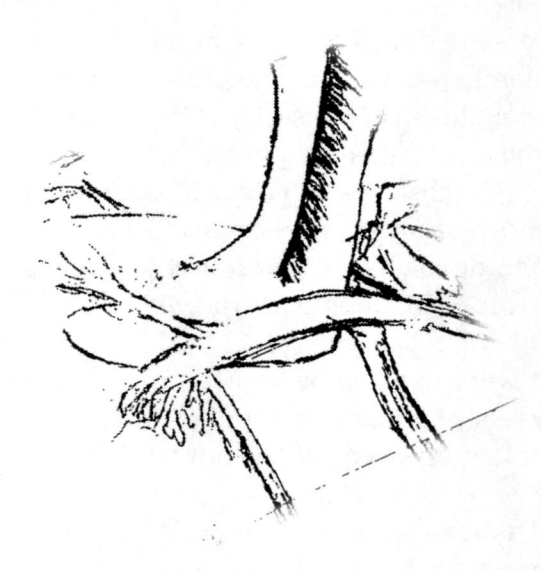

You tried not to make too many sounds because you knew there were certain animals that if they heard you, they would climb up and get to you!

"What did you do?" asked one of the young ones listening to the story." Grandfather replied, "You decided you were in trouble and needed some help."

"Then what?" said one of the young listeners.

"You asked the Great Spirit and He said in your mind, one word… "Wait." Wait? you said to yourself."

"Wait for what?" said the young listener. "You do not understand either? Your foot is hurting even more. What were you waiting for?" said Grandfather. (Grandfather always put his listener as the one that is in the story.)

"Even in the middle of the night the Great Spirit repeated the same word. "wait, wait" continued Grandfather.

"Your foot is throbbing with pain now, with every heart beat and beginning to swell, making it tighter and tighter between the two limbs.

By morning your foot and ankle had turned black and blue like the colors of the sunset.

Illustration by Glady Cobb

You had obeyed and waited all night, even though you thought of just falling out of that tree and maybe your foot would come loose when you fell to the ground.

Then a very strong wind blew, and shook the tree and the two limbs holding your foot pulled apart and released your foot."

"O it really hurt now! You are hanging by your arms but ware free. Tired but free. You carefully and slowly climbed down to the ground. You found a stick to use as a crutch and slowly limbed back toward your village. When you were close to the village, you called out and someone heard you. They came and you were carried into the village and to your home.

Daily, you were taken to the ice cold spring to soak your foot and daily you would cover your foot in honey first to help the cuts heal, and then with smelly buffalo grease to reduce the swelling. You had to hold it up most of the time to reduce the swelling and you could only walk short distances.

It took weeks for your foot to heal but "you will never forget that sometimes we have to be patient even when something hurts (like your feelings) and to obey the Great Spirit's words."

Then Grandfather showed some scars on his foot and we knew that he was the one that had got trapped in a tree. I had always wondered how he got those scars.

Illustration by Joan Shaw

Chapter Two

"Stay Over Night In The Desert"

I (Little Eagle) was sitting down next to Grandfather then he said, "Are you ready for your next journey toward becoming a scout?" I said nothing only nodding my head up and down.

Grandfather continued, "I want you to "stay overnight in the Desert."

I thought to myself, "This is going to be an easy test. I have stayed overnight in the woods before. Maybe this time I will not get into trouble."

I gathered some food, my knife, flint rocks that are used to start a fire, a blanket and my nice soft warm pillow made with rabbit fur skin and walked through the woods into the desert.

Illustration by Joan Shaw

I was saying to myself, "Easy Test," easy test, easy test." I picked a camping spot near a spring that I had found before that was hidden in the desert for water and rested. It was still daylight so I chased rabbits, looked for lizards and frogs, and played around the rest of the day.

Illustration by Glady Cobb

I was still thinking, easy test, easy test.

Then it began to sprinkle, then rain and then a real down pour. The rain soaked my blanket, my pillow and I got soaking wet! The sun went down and I was getting cold.

In the darkness, I heard…wolves howling in the distant mountains and the sounds were getting closer and closer. The wolves must be really hungry to leave the mountains in search of food. They must have been watching me or they smelled me. Now I could see shadows circling me in the distance and it was wolves.

I remembered what you should always do when you stay overnight in the woods or this time in the desert!

Build a fire...to keep the animals away!
I could hear the wolves are getting closer and closer and they continued to circle me.   All the wood, sticks, leaves and small logs that I had not gathered were now wet.

I now remembered that I should have started a fire to keep the animals away. Before when I had stayed over night in the woods, I had always built a fire. And now everything is wet.

I knew that I did not have enough food to feed all the wolves nor would I be able to keep them from attacking with my little knife.

I can hear the wolves growling and their paws walking over the sand and water puddles. Now the young pups are playing with me by nibbling at my ankles. But I could tell from the growling, that the Moms and Dad wolves were not playing around. Their stomachs were hurting and guess who was for supper! Me!

Illustration by Joan Shaw

I decided I was in trouble! I knew what Grandfather always said to do when you get into trouble… ask for help. I whispered to myself, "O Great Spirit; help me. The wolves are ready to attack."

I had learned from previous experiences that the Great Spirit will always answer and say only one or two or sometimes three words and this time…it was three words that I do not want to do!

No way do I want to obey these three words and besides I did not understand how obeying these three words would keep the wolves away?

The three words were…"Hug a Cactus!" Hug a cactus? The big wolves are still circling and the pups are still biting my ankles. But the moms and dads are ready to attack.

In the moon light (the rain had finally stopped and the sky had cleared) I could just barely see a large cactus nearby. I jumped over the wolves and ran over to that big tall cactus. I put my arms and legs around it and I felt hundreds of sharp needles digging into my arms and legs and stomach and face! I did not understand why the Great Spirit said, "Hug a cactus."

I stepped back and I had hundreds of those sharp cactus needles still stuck to my arms and legs and stomach and my face and I was bleeding. O my arms and legs and stomach and face hurt so much!

The Mom and Dad wolves moved in and attacked. Their mouths are open wide biting me on my arms, legs, arms and stomach and I was able to keep them from my face. I could see their sharp teeth and smell their bad breath as they also scratched me with their paws.
Then the hungry wolves jumped back and yelped loudly.

I did not understand until I saw hundreds of sharp needles sticking to their mouths and teeth and paws. The Great Spirit must have known something when I was told to hug a cactus. The wolves backed off growled and then yelped in pain. I was wet, cold, bleeding and hurting and still in trouble. I must find a shelter because I was wet and shivering in the cold and a cold wind began to blow.

Chapter Three

"Finding Shelter"

Illustration by Joan Shaw

I whispered again, O Great Spirit help me! I listened and was given three more words and even though I did not understand, I did not hesitate,"Clap Your Hands!" "Clap Your Hands!" I knew that my hand claps would not scare away the hungry wolves. In the darkness, I heard an echo. I clapped my hands three more times and the echo came from a certain direction in the darkness. The Great Spirit must be telling me to run toward the echo.

I leaped over the wolves and ran toward the echo with the wolves on my heels. I ran through the darkness lit only by the full moon just barely missing the cactus and the sticks and splashed through the water puddles.

In the darkness, I slammed into a cliff. I could hear the wolves thinking, "we have him trapped now." I felt a big opening in the cliff. It was a cave!

Illustration by Glady Cobb

I crawled into the cave with the wolves right behind me and I knew they were saying, "Finally we will get to eat!" But in the total darkness of the cave, guess what I found? I found some dry wood and some dry leaves, that someone had stored in the cave. I piled up the dry leaves then made a little teepee with small sticks then carefully added some larger and larger sticks of wood around the leaves and twigs.

I took the flint rocks out of my bag and hit them together. The sparks lit up the dark cave and scared the wolves back a little and so they backed away toward the cave opening. The hot flint chips dropped into the dry leaves and made them smolder, then catch a little fire, then the burning leaves made the larger sticks burn. Soon I could add even smaller logs, then larger logs, and they all began to burn.

Illustration by Joan Shaw

The wolves backed even further out when they saw the fire but guarded the front of the cave opening which was only a few feet away!

Every once in a while I would hit the flint rocks together to make sparks and the sounds would echo around the inside of the cave and scare the wolves and made them jump. I hollered at the wolves and said "Mr. Wolves, now you can stay put and pull out the needles from your paws, legs, mouths and teeth!" My words echoed many times inside the cave.

Chapter four

"Keeping the Wolves Out"
Falling Eagle story

Illustration by Joan Shaw

I soon had a nice bright warm fire to dry out everything including my clothes, moccasins and my fur blanket and rabbit pillow. I knew what I would have to do...

Illustration by Glady Cobb

Stay awake all night to keep the fire going so that it would keep the wolves out.

To keep awake I shouted out loud the stories of the "Falling Eagle," "Fast Turtle," and "Don't Speak With a Forked Tongue" and began to slowly pull out the cactus needles from my hands first.

(Would you like to hear the stories that kept Little Eagle awake as he was keeping the fire going to keep the wolves away?)

"The Falling Eagle" shouted Little Eagle in the direction of the hungry wolves.

"The earth is dying. The plants and animals are suffering and dying. The air is thick and smelly and the sunlight is red and dark and cold. There is a little eagle looking down at the earth below from a high cliff. He had climbed that cliff to get closer to the sun so that he could get warm. But the sun is cold and dark and he is cold. He looks down at the rivers below and they are muddy and poisoned and filled with dead fish and dead animals and trash.

Illustration by Joan Shaw

The little eagle is crying because he is alone. His family has died leaving him all by himself and now there was no one left. He is choking as he is breathing the filthy polluted air.

Illustration by Joan Shaw

He jumps off that cliff and flies upward in bigger and bigger circles higher and higher to get closer and closer to the sun to try to get warm. Then the air disappears and he is choking, he cannot breathe. The sun disappears, and it is pitch black and he is falling, falling and falling. He flaps his wings as hard as he can but there is no air…

The following Illustrations are by Joan Shaw

*The following Illustrations
are by Joan Shaw*

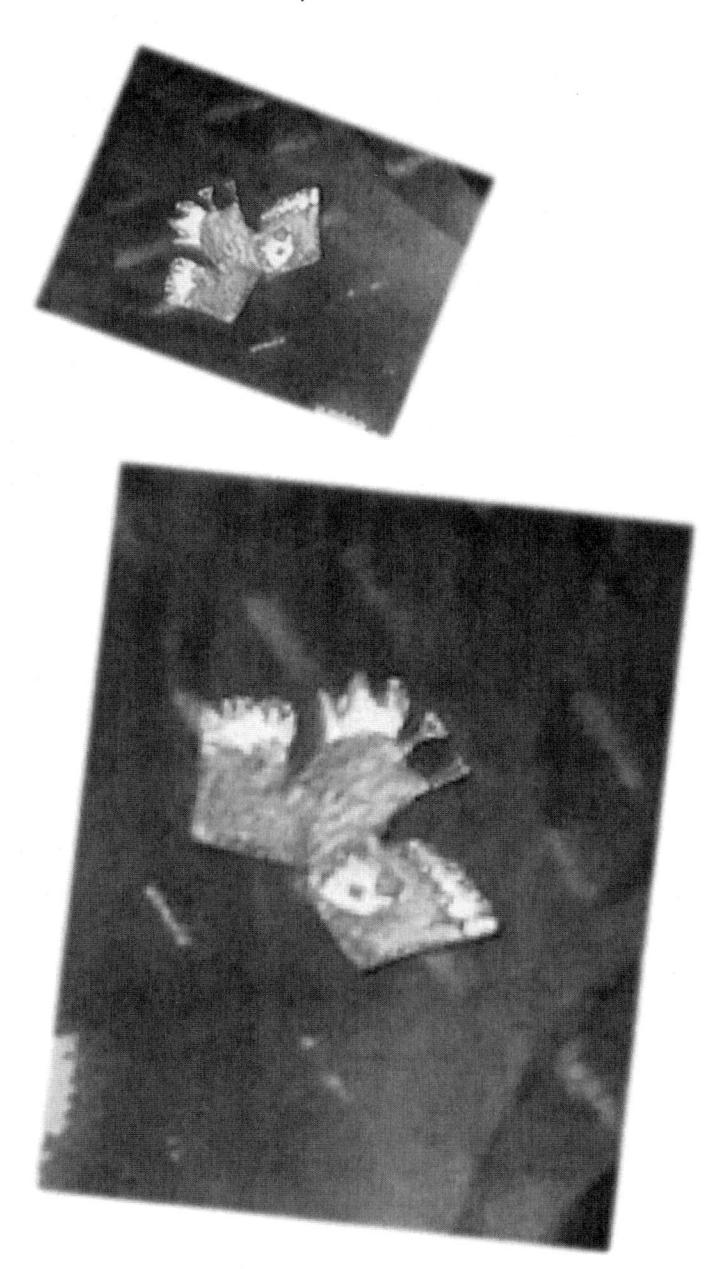

Then the Great Spirit says to his son, "It is time for a new earth and a new creation, but we have left behind this little eagle. He is flapping his wings and suffocating and falling and scared and confused.

Hurry, we must create a new earth for him. So, a big rock is formed and a new sun is formed and it brightens and warms up the falling eagle. But the little eagle now sees this big rock below and he is falling toward that big rock.

Then the Great Spirit says "Hurry we must make water and plants so that the little eagle will have something to drink and new air made by the plants to keep him from suffocating and smashing into the new earth. Hurry we must create soil for the rock and for the new plants and new animals and clean water the new rock.

So water and soil and plants are made on the rock and the plants create new clean air for the rock. The little eagle now can breathe and he feels his wings lifting his body up and he is flying again.

But he is still falling and he looks down and sees that he is falling toward a large cat that will now catch him and eat him. He is now so tired from flapping his wings that he cannot fly away from the mouth of the big cat.

Illustration by Christina Blum

The Great Spirit said "Hurry we must create man to catch our little eagle and keep him safe." So man and woman are created and catches the little eagle and puts him back up on another high cliff.

The little eagle opens his eyes and sees a beautiful new earth with new water, new plants and new animals and everything is bright with a new warm sun and new air.

Illustration by Joan Shaw

He is so happy. He jumps off the cliff and flies in greater and greater circles and calls out with a loud screeching happy sounds to celebrate the new sky, new sun, new water, new animals and new creation below. And so today when you hear the screeching sounds of an eagle, remember this story.

Illustration by Joan Shaw

Little Eagle throw some more wood on the fire and said to himself, "I must stay awake, keep the fire going and I will keep hitting my flint rocks and making sparks so the wolves will know that I am not sleeping." So, I shouted out another story.

Chapter five

"Fast Turtle"
Told to me by Chief Leaford Bearskin
Of the Wyandotte Nation*

"Some boys were making fun of you because you were smaller and shorter and not as strong as them. This really hurt your feelings. Grandfather asked if he could talk with you by yourself at the old tree stump. He whispered this story, but I am shouting this story, "Do you hear me Mr. Wolves?"

"Animals talk to each other as you know. This is about a turtle slowly walking around this lake. He was so happy as a turtle and he was enjoying nature sights and sounds. As he was walking, along came a fox.. The fox came to the turtle and said,

Illustration by Glady Cobb

"Mr. Turtle. You move so slow and your legs are so short, it will take you a long time to go around this lake, he was just making fun of Mr. Turtle. Mr. Turtle thought for a moment and said, "Well Mr. Fox, do you see that island in the middle of this lake?

Illustration by Joan Shaw

I will race you to that island." Mr. Fox laughed and laughed and knowing that he was much bigger and could swim much faster than Mr. Turtle. "OK, I will race you to that island" said Mr. Fox, knowing that he could make even more fun of Mr. Turtle when he got to the island.

So, Mr. Turtle and Mr. Fox jumped into the lake and swam as fast as they could to win the race. But guess who was waiting for Mr. Fox when he got to the island? Yes, there was Mr. Turtle sitting there waiting for him! Mr. Fox did not understand but did not make fun of Mr. Turtle again.

Next day, here was Mr. Turtle just enjoying nature sights and sounds and walking around the lake so happy that he was a turtle. And along came a bear. The bear watched Mr. Turtle and finally said,

Illustration by Clark Harp
Illustration by
Clark Harp

"Mr. Turtle. You move so slow and your legs are so short it will take you a long time to go around this lake." Just making fun of Mr. Turtle. Mr. Turtle thought for a moment and replied, "Well Mr. Bear. do you see that island in the middle of this lake? I will race you to that island."

Mr. Bear laughed and laughed and knew that he was much bigger and could swim much faster than Mr. Turtle.
"OK, Mr. Turtle, I will race you to that island," knowing that he would make even more fun of Mr. Turtle when he got to the island first."

So, Mr. Turtle and Mr. Bear jumped into the lake and swam as fast as they could to win the race. But guess who was waiting for Mr. Bear when he got to the island? Yes, it was Mr. Turtle sitting there waiting for him!   Mr. Bear did not understand so he did not make more fun of Me. Turtle.

The next day, there was Mr. Turtle just enjoying nature sights and sounds and walking around the lake so happy that he was a turtle.   An along came Mr. Beaver.   Mr. Beaver watched Mr. Turtle and finally said, "Mr. Turtle. You move so slow and your legs are so short it will take you a long time to go around this lake." He was just making fun of Mr. Turtle.

Mr. Turtle thought for a moment and replied, "Well Mr. Beaver. I am kind of tired today, but do you see that island in the middle of the lake? Tomorrow, I will race you to that island."   Mr. Beaver laughed and laughed just making fun of Mr. Turtle and thinking to himself, I know I am faster and can beat him and then I will make more fun of his short legs and how he moves so slow" and walked away knowing that he will challenge Mr. Turtle tomorrow.

Then Mr. Turtle walked slowly up to the edge of the lake, jumped in and swam to the bottom of that lake and met...his twin brother Mr. Turtle II. They both swam to the island and "laughed and laughed inside" and how they fooled Mr. Fox and Mr. Bear and who ever might make fun of them.

Grandfather said, "Don't make fun of any one because they are different. Just be happy for who you are. And when someone makes fun of you just remember this story. You see, I am a twin myself." said grandfather "and we used to switch places and not let any one know and then we would "laugh inside" knowing what we had done in secret!" And we never made fun of anyone because they were different. Just be glad for who you are" and remember Mr. Fast Turtle."

(Chief Leaford Bearskin had a twin brother just like your author who also has a twin brother and both of us used to switch places.)

Illustration by Joan Shaw

*Chief Leaford Bearskin's book, "Kwa-hoo-sha-ha-ke" American Indian Warrior Hero, A glimpse into the life of Leaford Bearskin, Chief of the Wyandotte Nation.

(Author's note: As I was visiting with Leaford we were reflecting on native history. Because of his extensive military background retiring as a Lieutenant Colonel, I will always remember his perspective, "You can't march forward, by looking backward.")

Little Eagle threw some more wood on the fire to let the wolves know that he had not fallen asleep.

"I sang and shouted another story that Grandfather told me when I did not tell the truth. When I only gave part of the answer when I was asked what I had done.

I had found some water in the cave and got a drink and continued to pull cactus needles out from my face, arms, stomach and legs while I was telling the next story, "Don't Speak With A Forked Tongue."

I carefully washed the poison out of each hole that was left in my arms, legs, stomach and face because cactus needles all have poisons from the plants around them.

Even though each needle hurt when I pulled them out, I did not let the wolves know. I found some honey in my food bag and put that on the wounds and ate the remaining dry meat, apples and nuts that I had.

I could tell that the wolves were smelling this food and I could hear them whimpering so I threw some of my food out toward the young ones. I found some shells that someone had left in the cave and filled them up with water and carefully placed them at the cave entrance.

I had to keep the fire small so that the smoke would not drive me out of the cave. I added only a small number of wood sticks to the fire at any time so that hopefully would have enough wood until dawn.

Illustration by Joan Shaw

Chapter six

"Don't Speak With A Forked Tongue"
(Also told to me by Chief Leaford Bearskin Of the Wyandotte Nation)

Illustration by Glady Cobb

There were four young natives who lived in this village in long houses like the Choctaw rather than in teepees. The nations that lived in teepees traveled and it was easy to carry and set up teepees. But some nations like the Choctaw were planters and they lived for a while in a place and shared their food with their neighbors.

Illustration by Joan Shaw

(Grandfather always wanted to add more to the stories each time he told them.) The natives in this village heard from their Grandfather about this old man in the mountains that would grant any wish, by asking the Great Spirit.

So, they traveled a long time and many miles to get to the top of this mountain and found the old man. The first native said to the old native of the mountain,

"I am a good hunter. I can find game and shoot straight and gather much food for my village. "What is your wish, the Old man said to the first visitor.

"I wish that I will never lose my skills as a hunter and never let my village go hungry, even when I get old like you."

The Old Man said, "I will go to the Great Spirit and see if the Great Spirit will grant you your wish.? After a while the he came back and said, "You speak the truth, you are a great hunter and you do find much game and you have never let your village go hungry. The Great Spirit said I shall grant you your wish. You will never lose your skills as a hunter and always find game and you will never let your village go hungry for the rest of your life." The young native went away so happy.

The Old Man said, "What is it that you would like to say? To the second native visitor. "I am a good Scout. I know how to find ways and water and shelter in the woods and the deep forests and lead my friends from one place to another so that they will never get lost." What is your wish? Said the old native.

"I wish that I will always have the ability to be a good scout and always find good paths to follow and fresh water and will never let my friends get lost when they travel with me." The old native said, "I will go to the Great Spirit and see if the Great Spirit will grant you your wish. And the second young native waited.

Soon the old native returned and said, "You are a good scout, you always find good paths to follow and water for those that you lead through the woods and forests.

Illustration by Joan Shaw

You speak the truth so the Great Spirit will grant you your wish. You will always be a good scout and find good paths and good water and you will never get anyone lost in the woods and forest, even to the rest of your life!" The second native went away so happy that his wish had been granted.
"What is your purpose for coming?" the old one said to the third visitor. "I am a good warrior, the best warrior." said the third visitor. "I know how to protect my people and I have the skills to fight man or animal as a warrior. I know how to make the best bows and arrows and hatchets and I can shoot great distances." "What is it that you wish for?" said the Old One. "I wish to never lose these skills as a warrior so that I may protect my village all of my life."

"I will go to the Great Spirit and ask." Said the Old One. After waiting a long time, the old native came back and he said, "You speak the truth, you are a good warrior and you have many skills to protect your village and you can make good bows and straight arrows and sharp arrow points. The Great Spirit will grant you your wish." The third visitor went away so happy.

What is it that you want to wish for? He said to the last visitor. "I am a great hunter and a great scout and a great warrior." Said the fourth visitor.

Illustrations by Joan Shaw

"What do you wish for?" said the Old One to the last visitor.

My wish is to live forever," said the last native visitor.

"I will ask the Great Spirit and the Old native went away.. The young native waited and waited and waited a long time. The old native did not come back until the next day, but when he came he said,

"The Great Spirit say that you lie! You are not a good hunter or a good scout nor a great warrior! You speak with a forked tongue. You are not telling the truth."

"But...the Great Spirit will grant you your wish!" said the Old One.

The young native was so happy that he would get his wish to live forever. The old native then touched the fourth visitor lightly on the shoulder and...
...the young native...
...turned into a...rock!
And a rock lives forever.

Grandfather then pointed to a nearby cliff...

Illustration by Glady Cobb

Can you make out the rough side view of a head in the left side of the cliff face looking out over mother earth? Can you make out an eye and a nose and a sad mouth?

"We can pretend that that is the native that got his wish to live forever and to help you remember this story." Said Grandfather.

"Always tell the truth. Even if you are tempted to tell only part of the truth or to make up something that is not true or tell something that is false."

I will always remember the story "Don't Speak With A Forked Tongue"

I shouted again toward the wolves at the doorway to the cave, "Remember what the Great Spirit said Mr. Wolves! And remember the story of the fast turtle and to take care of mother earth in the falling eagle story and to always tell the truth!"

Just then I noticed that sunlight was entering the door way of the cave. The wolves were gone! I filled up my water bag with spring water from the cave, put out the fire and picked up one small burnt stick.

I put it into my pocket and left the cave. I looked back over the desert and I could now see the cactus that was missing some needles near the bottom and walked into the village still covered with needles and sat down by Grandfather just when the sun lifted up over the mountains. I told my story and gave Grandfather the burnt stick and gave some of the cave spring water to the children. I even gave some of the longer needles to the women to be used for sewing leather. I was stilling pulling out the smaller needles from my face and arms and stomach and legs. Grandfather put his hand lightly on my shoulder and said,

"Little Eagle you have passed all of your tests toward becoming a scout. Look what the village family has put on a blanket down by the fire…"

Illustration by Glady Cobb

My stomach was really hurting and the food on the blanket tasted so good…

Grandfather told me to rest up that night because the next day I would receive one of Grandfather's eagle feathers as their village scout.

Illustration by Glady Cobb

That night I dreamed about being a scout and what I would do as a scout and I could see myself leading many friends through the woods, forests, deserts and mountains so that they would not get lost. And I thanked the Great Spirit for helping me twice on this last journey when I was "attacked by wolves."

I had trouble sleeping and in my mind, I reviewed another one of Grandfather's stories called, "Follow The River."

Chapter seven

"Follow the river"

You remembered that you had asked Grandfather to help you decide what you wanted to do in your life. After visiting with you, you told him about the many hard things that had happened to you and that you did not understand why. Grandfather sat for a while and didn't say a word and then finally,

Grandfather said, "Are you willing to follow this river to the beginning of the river and back to the village? On this journey you will learn something from the Great Spirit about life."

Illustration by Glady Cobb

So, you started just when the sun got up, walking upstream. It was easy to follow the river. But soon the river went "this way and that way" like a rabbit runs and you had to walk a long way as you were following the shore.

Then the shore got real muddy and deep and it was harder to follow the river. You thought, "I will just cut across and not have to travel so far. I will just go around all this mud and still be following the river."

But you remembered what Grandfathers had said, "Follow the river." You did not cut across but remained close to the bank even though it was hard.

Then the river went by cliffs and bluffs and you had to climb up and down as you stayed by the river. You wanted to go around the cliffs and bluff. You reasoned it would be longer and take more time but easier.

Grandfather didn't say anything about cliffs and bluffs? Then there were flooded areas and sticky, dirty, muddy areas.

Illustration by Christina Blum

Then there were so many sticker bushes and thorns along the shore and you got covered with stickers and dirty mud and you lost your moccasins when you pulled out your feet from the deep mud. Your clothes are now torn and shredded and your skin cut and split open. And you are covered with stains from the poison berries and hickory thorns.

Illustration by Glady Cobb

You thought, "This is not worth it, I am going to turn around and go back the shortest way possible. I will just tell Grandfather that I actually did get to the beginning of the river and actually did follow it back to the village."

But you remembered the "Forked Tongue" story and continued to follow the bank of the river. Soon the river got very narrow and you found that the river was fed by a huge spring of fresh water. You filled your water bag and turned around and again followed the river back down stream toward your village barefoot and very tired now.

The sun was going down and it was getting darker and you walked and climbed the cliffs again as fast as you could. Since you were bare foot you tried to find your moccasins by wading through the mud with your feet and reaching down in the mud with your hands.

Illustration by Glady Cobb

You slowly and carefully went back through the sticker bushes and through the shallow areas.

It was hard and you were getting very tired and very sore and very scratched and your cuts hurt even more. You were very troubled because you kept repeating "The Great Spirit will teach you about life.'

You went back through the poison bushes, and poison ivy and red rose bushes and your skin was covered with sharp thorns and purple and blue and red stains.

You thought, "I can see where I could still cut across and not have to go through this torcher. Grandfather would not know. "This is not worth it" you shouted out loud. You had great difficulty climbing back over the cliffs again and walking over rocks in your bare feet.

Illustration by Glady Cobb and Christina Blum respectively.

Your skin was itching and your stomach hurting, and your eyes swollen and you were bleeding.

When you finally reached your village, you had to be carried. They laid you down by Grandfather and you were "crying on the inside," where it would not show.

"What did you learn today," said Grandfather. You answered and said, "I do not understand what the Great Spirit wanted me to learn from this terrible experience.

"I will have scars for life and these stains will never disappear and I have sores all over from poison ivy and poison oak and poison berries and the mud has infected my cuts and I feel sick."

You continued. "All I found was a big spring where the river starts. I do not understand, what was it that I was supposed to learn?

Grandfather slowly took a drink of the remaining water that you had left in your water bag for him and said,

"The Great Spirit is like this river. Sometimes it is easy to follow and to stay close to it. And sometimes it is very difficult to remain faithful and remember that it exists. It would have been very easy for you to have left the river or left the Great Spirit."

"It would have been easy to just "cut across" or "leave the Great Spirit behind," or "give up." But I know that you have been faithful. You did follow the river even when it got real hard and really difficult. You brought back the very best water that I know came from the big spring that starts this river. Water that tastes better than any water downstream tastes. I know you followed the river," said Grandfather.

After a long moment he continued, "You have the same scars and cuts and stains on your face, arms, legs and feet that I have." We all struggle to keep the Great Spirit in our lives, and to remain close to that Great Spirit even though it would be easy to leave it and find our own path." This is what you were to learn. Look what your village family have prepared for you…all kinds of food!" finished Grandfather.

It took days for your hurts and cuts to heal and you still see the scars and the purple and red stains on your legs and arms. And that's the story of "follow the river."

I had always wondered how Grandfather had gotten these stains and scars and cuts in his legs, arms, hands and face.

Little Eagle had gone to sleep sometime as he was reviewing the story and finally woke up and as he was getting ready for the ceremony. He remembered the ten journeys that he took to be ready for today.

Grandfather called all the village to come. "Beat the drum and sing and eat, because Little Eagle will become our scout today. Finally, at sunset just when the sun shadows were going down the teepees and as the fire was glowing brighter, Grandfather asked Little Eagle to sit beside him. He waited until the sun had disappeared and then took one of his eagle feathers from his head band and reached over to Little Eagle and,

Illustration by Gwen Wirth-Lind

gave him one of his biggest eagle feathers and said to all the village,

"Little Eagle has gotten a piece of rabbit fur, grew corn plants as tall as mine, faithfully followed the trail that I had marked. He has gotten attacked by an eagle while getting a feather from an eagle." I tied a piece of leather over his eyes and I took him deep in the woods and he was to find his way back but he got lost but he found his way back.

Little Eagle was able to get a piece of fur from a live black bear and then to find something to eat in the woods when all the animals had eaten the food. It took Little Eagle many days to chase his pony and he and his pony ended up sick in the desert.

Then his pony ran away just before he got back in the middle of the night but his pony came back to him because Little Eagle was his friend. He walked into our villages with his pony without tying the rope around the pony's neck.

Little Eagle almost drowned swimming back across our river when I knew it was going to rain and the river would flood and now when he has been attacked by wolves in the desert he found a cave and came back covered with cactus needles." He is now our village scout.

Little Eagle carefully fastened the eagle feather firmly into his head band. The children wanted to hear just one more story from Grandfather so he told the beautiful valley story.

Chapter eight
"The Beautiful Valley"

The village Grandfather asked this young couple, who had been wrapped in a marriage blanket, to go into the desert toward the rising sun and to take three days of food and they would learn something from the Great Spirit during this adventure.

They traveled for three days and ran out of food. They wondered, what did the Great Spirit want them to learn? On the fifth day, their stomachs were hurting. They and their ponies needed food and water they were getting sick. Just as they walked over a sand dune, they saw a beautiful green valley. It had all the food and game and water they needed.

They and their ponies enjoyed the valley so much that the boy said, "Let's stay here for the rest of our lives. We have everything we need."

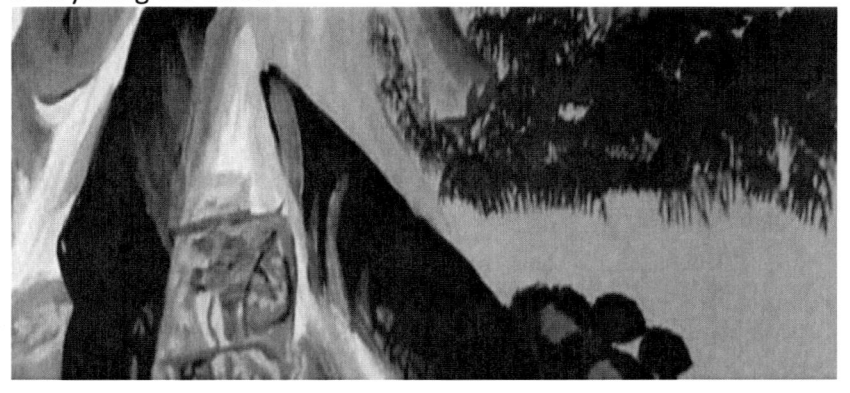

Illustration by Joan Shaw

The young girl, while looking into the fire, was already lonesome for her family and her village family and she knew that he needed to get back because he was the village scout. Both of them wondered what it was that the Great Spirit was supposed to teach them?

In her mind that night, she silently asked the Great Spirit what it was that they needed to learn? The Great Spirit whispered to her and said four words...that she did not understand. "We are only visitors."

"We are only visitors?" She remembered the four words. The next morning the boy whistled for his pony and his pony did not come. He found that his pony had died or as the natives say, "changed worlds" overnight.
The boy was heartbroken and she felt bad too.

Illustration by Christina Blum

He said, "I thought that I would always have my pony for the rest of my life. The girl said the Great Spirit told me four words last night and I do not understand? Let's go back to Grandfather and ask him." They gathered all the food they would need and traveled back on her pony.

They sat down by Grandfather and finally he said, "I see that you came back on one pony." They told about running out of food and finding a beautiful valley hiding in the desert. The wind would come up this valley and drop all kinds of moisture for the gardens in this valley.

Illustration by Joan Shaw

He told about his pony passing away and how sad he was. She then said, "I asked the Great Spirit what was it that we were to learn? Then one night the Great Spirit said four words.

Then Grandfather stopped her story and said, "I know what the Great Spirit said, "We are only visitors, right?" "Yes, and we do not understand." said the young girl.

Grandfather was silent for a while and then replied softly, "Well, we do not own anything, the trees, or grass or game or even the air we breathe. And Little Eagle, you did not own your pony.

Your pony was just a visitor too. And someday I will only be a memory because you see, I am only a visitor too. Think about this tonight.".

"Did the guy forget that he was the village scout?" Asked the children.

"Yes, he did. He was enjoying all the food and water and game in the beautiful valley that he forgot. He also, did not since how lonesome his girl was, for her own family and her village family." Grandfather spoke in his teaching voice.

When Grandfather finished the story and told the ending, he could tell that some of the children did not understand. Little Eagle remembered that when he first heard this story from Grandfather that he did not understand either but he understood now.

We all asked if Grandfather would tell one more story before he went to his teepee. He paused for the longest time, took a drink of water and said, "Do you remember what the Great Spirit said in the story of the healer with blue eyes? Everyone pretended that they had forgotten and wanted him to tell the story again.

Chapter Nine

"Healer With Blue Eyes"

"All the adults in this village were getting sick and they were getting weaker and weaker. The children met and talked it over, "What should we do? Even our chief and village council and the Medicine Man (or spiritual leader) are sick and dying, "

The young village scout said, "We are all in trouble." Let's ask the Great Spirit for some help." So together (without speaking out loud) they said in their minds, O Great Spirit help us.".

They all listened and in their mind they heard, "Look to the East at sunrise." They discovered that the Great Spirit had said the same words to all of the children and to the village scout. They all wondered what the Great Spirit meant?

So each morning the children would meet at the lake shore to watch the morning sunrise. By now they were all hungry and getting weak themselves and afraid that they too would get sick.

"Look to the east at sunrise."

One foggy morning, they saw a figure in a canoe out across their lake coming across the water. When the figure was closer they could see that it was a person paddling a stone canoe coming across the lake toward them.

When the fog lifted from over the lake, they could see that the person was wearing a beautiful long white leather jacket. They watched Him land on the shore and silently walk into their village.

The visitor carefully went to each sick person, he placed his hand on them and whispered some words to each one. Then He came over to the children and the young scout and looked at them and silently walked over to the stone canoe.

The children noticed that he had blue eyes. He got into his stone canoe and whispered "I will return" and paddled out across the lake and disappeared. The next day all the adults felt better and soon they were all healed.

The children and village scout said, "What did the healer whisper to you?" It was the same words that they had heard in their minds before He had come, "Look to the east. The adults were also told "I will come again. "

The village people all took up the stakes out of the ground holding down their teepees and turned the teepees around so that the door was facing east. And to this day that tribe always set up their doorways facing to the east and opened the flaps for just a few moments just before sunrise in memory of the "Healer With Blue Eyes."

Even today when that tribe builds their "homes" they always have one door facing east. Grandfather let the children go to their homes.

Little Eagle went to his teepee and dreamed as a scout a person that takes families through the woods, forest, desert and mountains so the they would not get lost.

Little did he know that even as a scout he would still get into trouble and need some help in the books, "Trapped on a Cliff," and "Snake Bit."

And that he would meet a native girl by the name of White Dove and build a rope bridge near her cliff village.

Illustration by Joan Shaw

Then he and white dove would get run over by buffalo and caught in a prairie fire, would be drowning in a flash flood. Both of them and a family would get trapped by a bear on a mountain side and he would almost freeze to death in a blizzard.

They would both get "Lost In The Fog," at night with a family and he would watch White Dove walk into deep mud and get trapped when she goes into the muddy valley after her beautiful white pony.

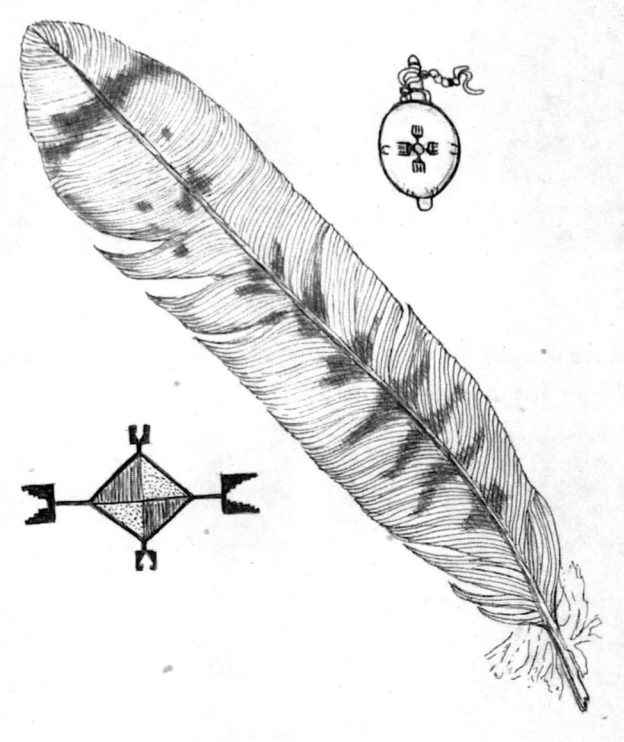

Illustration by Joan Shaw

Chapter Ten

"From your author"

-Mini Table of Contents-
The Perfect Man story..p. 54
When I took our family to visit the Navajo..........p. 57
The Pointing pole, a Choctaw Migration story......p.60
A town called Tahoka...p.62
A few things that I recall.....................................p. 64
Intro. to the "My White Dove" ....p. 65
Intro. to "Run Over by Buffalo"...........................p. 71
Intro. To "Caught in a Flash Flood"......................p. 75
Intro. To "White Dove Catch Your Pony"............p.76
Intro. To future Stories..p.81
End notes and pictures..p. 82

The first story that I collected was the only one told by my father. A story that I did not believe until I found the same general story in a book written with stories from the Chippewa nation in Michigan.

I forget now what book I found the story in years ago in the library in Mt. Pleasant, Michigan as one of the legends of the Chippewa Nation.

There were two stories that my full blood Choctaw father shared with us that I did not believe. The story of when he served in the National Guard and the "Perfect Man." He said that he and other National guard troops were put on a bus and taken to some county fair. He remembered that they were ordered to stand in a circle, fully armed, around a plane and guard it. He remembered that the plane had a strange name painted on the side, "Spirit of Saint Louis." He had no idea that that plane had flown across the ocean by someone called Charles Lindberg. Apparently, that plane was shown in many places in those days. My father had no idea that he was a part of the history of that plane.

> "When the Perfect man was created."

My father was not a storyteller so when he told this story about creation, I did not put much weight on it.

My father said, "The Great Spirit said to his Son, it is time to create the perfect man." So, the Great Spirit mixed up some mud and formed a human with His hands and put it over the campfire. The Great Spirit had some other things to do and was gone too long. Now the first man was over-cooked and came out kind of black. The Great Spirit said, "I left this first man over the fire too long. I love him and will keep him." He placed this "over cooked man" in a land all his own that we now call Africa."

The Great Spirit said, "Let us make another man." So He mixed up some more mud and formed another man and again placed it over the campfire. This time He watched over his man and got worried and… pulled the man out of the campfire too soon. This man was "half-baked" and "kind of white." My father said He said, "We did not leave him over the campfire long enough, I love him and will keep him." He placed that man in the area we call Europe today.

"Let us make one more man," said the Great Spirit."

So another figure was made out of mud and put over the campfire again. He knew that the first person was left too long over the campfire and the second person was left not long enough, so He pulled mud figure out "just in time." "Now that is the perfect man, it's nice and brown." We will place him in what we call North America.

And of course, my father would end telling this story and say, "That is Native Americans." Of course, we didn't believe the story even when we were very young. But when I sit down with the children I always mention what my father always said, "If you have been born in the United States, then you are a native American" so that I try to get the point across that you are a native if you are born in the United States. I do not tell the above story.

When I sit down on a blanket in front of hundreds of children and one asks, "Little Eagle. Are these stories true?" I always respond by saying, "When I heard these stories, I asked the same question to the many tribal leaders when they shared their traditions. They would say, Well, we don't know if any of these stories are true, but what we do know this story is true. But they have been told for many years and they still help children learn about the Great Spirit.

Along with my full blood father, I never felt that I or my father or any of our relatives were anyone special. I remember asking him, "When will I become a full blood Choctaw?"

I did not know that my father was native until he took our family to visit the Williston's in southern Oklahoma. When he said we were going to see Indians, I remember being afraid! Because the only image I had of Indians were in the movies and being hit by arrows and being attacked by Indians in John Wayne movies.

When I became a teacher, I had the summers to work or to travel to collect stories. I had decided to just travel to various native nations to find out about how they taught their children about their word for God which was the Great Spirit. I found out that every native nation (I do not use the term tribe because that was a derogatory term introduced by those that came across the water) had stories and I wanted to collect the stories about the "Great Spirit" involvement in their lives.

When I heard the stories they were "way too long" for children of today and of course they had different names for the natives who were in the stories. So, I had to shorten them and gave my native name as the main character. Sometimes I am asked if I had to pass any of these experiences. (I called them tests). I would say, "as I was growing up (and even now) I had harder tests to pass on my journey with the "Great Spirit."

Some of my tests were the struggle of leaving out cuss words or profanity from my vocabulary. There were times when I was "pushed" by others (gangs and even friends) to steal and to do damage or fight to break into a house or to fight when I was bullied or made fun of. As a six grader, my brother and I learned "self-defense" the "art-of-getting-away" when grabbed or when someone was forcing us to get into a fight. It was a way to deal with those who push you or grab you and hit you.

 Over the many years of visiting schools I was often asked who the Great Spirit is, I would always say, "Oh it just another name for God."

To visit the Navajo in Arizona.

On my very first trip to a native reservation I decided to take our family. My plan was to just pick out a village and gather the children and parents and tell stories. I remembered as a child when our family visited various native nations, my mother would pull out her auto-harp and begin to sing and the children would come. I didn't have that old auto-harp.

Our church gave us some money for this journey and I wanted to spend it wisely and to have a good experience for our family. We had a long weekend to travel over 1000 miles one way. I was hoping for a good adventure for our pre-teens and certainly my wife Nancy who we discovered later, had native blood with the Chippewa of Michigan.

We had a long week end. We traveled all night so the children could sleep. We would just find a village and sit down together with the children and visit, or maybe sing songs, or maybe just visit. Because at that I time had no stories that I wanted to tell.

We get to a large city outside of the Navajo reservation and it begins to rain. And rain it did, all weekend it rained. And now there were no roads that could be traveled on to any village, because their roads had turned to deep mud. I thought to myself, "Thanks a lot!" now we are trapped in this motel with nowhere to go.

It was a Friday night and we found out that the natives who had come to town had no way to get back to their villages and had decided to have a "pow wow" in the local gym. I said to the family, "Let's go and see what happens." Being a Choctaw we did not have the tradition of what is called a "pow wow."

The Choctaw were scouts, farmers, storytellers and singers, present and in the past. The Choctaw were not placed on a reservation because we were not a waring nation, so I had no idea what a reservation was.

On the way to the Navajo pow wow and even before we left home, I had heard noises from the water pump in our big station wagon. So I had put tools in and brought another water pump in the car, just in case...

At the pow wow we met a young teenager named Larry, (who was a member of the same church that helped finance this trip). We "felt" the vibration of the Navajo drum, watched them dance and sing and we accepted their invitation to join them in the "welcome dance."

Sure enough, on the way back to the motel, in the rain, the water pump died and the motor got really hot.

When we settled down for the night I knew what I had to do the next day...find a garage to get the old water pump out and replace it with the used one that I thoughtfully had brought with us.

It was Saturday and no open garages could be found. I was under the hood working in the down pouring rain, tearing out all the stuff just to get to the old water pump, when Larry came by.

He asked if he could help. "Thank-you" I said and he did help that morning, under the hood, in the pouring down windy rain. We got the water pump changed and I asked Larry," what can I pay you for your help? Larry finally said, "My aunt is in the hospital dying of cancer and I would like to see her one more time. The hospital is many miles away...but on a main highway."

By this time the kids and Nancy were really bored being "trapped" in the motel on our adventure of a lifetime to visit the Indians!

"Sure, we can take you, I said with a smile." He had two other friends who wanted to go and we all piled into our station wagon and after a few hours we got to the hospital. Larry said, "Why don't you come and meet my family" (he had recognized their cars in the parking lot).

"Sure" I said.

In the waiting room, Larry introduced his father who happened to be the chief of his village called "Twisted Water" and also their spiritual leader commonly called "Medicine Man." Larry also introduced us to his mother and his grandparents and others. They all thanked us for bringing Larry. Then Larry's grandmother said, "Come and visit us."

I said, "I'm teaching school and have to be back Monday. I will come at another time." I thought inside, "We didn't accomplish anything on this trip." Why did it rain?"

On the next visit, I found out that the tradition for the Navajo for visitors, that it was very important that they receive "an invitation" from first the Grandmother of the village, then the medicine man and then the chief."

Because it rained, because of the pow wow, because we met with Larry, because the car broke down because we brought him to the hospital and met his family, we had received "an invitation" and I was welcomed on future visits.

On one of those visits, I was flown in a "pieced together" airplane, (by a pilot whose hobby was to find used parts from different airplanes and put them together). I was able to share and learn stories at an all-night storytelling, to fly with the children in the airplane I called "the eagle," and to study their gardens and to visit other Navajo towns.

I learned much later that Larry had committed suicide. I never knew why.

I was introduced to the life on a reservation. Each nation had a council and leader, their own law enforcement, their own laws and rules. When one crosses the reservation line then the ones on the next reservation are in charge. I learned about the effects of alcohol, dependence on welfare, and finding jobs outside the reservation. I also found out their children were taken away and not seen again.

I learned how each village had a plan for every person for jobs that needed to be done. They had a plan to corral their sheep in certain areas and that area would be their garden the following year. On one visit, I had discovered their source of water was up in the mountains and I suggested that the spring could be capped and gravity feed the water to their village. The chief said, "No because everyone has a job and a schedule for going to the spring and getting water.

I was asked by the various story tellers to not have their name or nation mentioned so I have called them Grandfather stories except for Chief Bearskin's "Fast Turtle," and "Don't Speak with forked tongue."

"The Pointing Pole"
When I sat down with the elders, I am always curious about what they know about their migrations. Many native nations

were forced to move from their homelands. I am one/half Choctaw and spent some time and travels to interview various Choctaw elders about our tribe's history. I wanted to focus on where we came from and how we ended up in Southeastern Oklahoma. The Choctaw now number over 200,000 and can be found all over.

I sat down with a Choctaw elder, Charlie Jones and he painted a picture of what he knew about the Choctaw migrations… Two twins Chocah and Chicah were told by the Great Spirit that it was time for their people to move.

They were to put a pole in the ground and the next day it would point to the direction for them to go. It would point generally to the northeast. Chocah and Chicah would find water and game along the way for the hundreds of people that they were leading.

From the mountains which they loved, and now into the desert. Somewhere in the desert, the pole would not point, which meant that they would be staying for a while. Chocah and Chicah found a lake but when they tasted it "it was salty." "Tah Oka" which meant bad water. The Great Spirit said, "go around the lake and search."

They found a nice spring that fed the lake and stayed for some time until the pole pointed again. This time, mostly, to the east north east. They came to a wide river, which they called "Mississippi" which means in Choctaw, wide or big river.

The two brothers separated on the banks of that river and Chicah went north into what is now Oklahoma and they became known as Chickasaw. Chocah took the remaining nation across the river and ended up in the middle of what is now called the state of Mississippi where they stayed north of what is now Jackson and in a community now called "Philadelphia."

They were then moved in the 1830's on a "trail of tears," into southeast Oklahoma where they are now. Chocah's people became known as the Choctaw. Both nations today have a similar original language.

A Texas Town by the name of Tahoka

I was always wanting to verify this history. For a number of years, I was invited to make author visits to a number of schools in and around Lubbock Tx.

Just South of Lubbock was a town by the name of Tahoka. I visited with some of the town elders about the history of their town. They said, "Well, before the town had a name, there was an Indian tribe that came here and stayed awhile and then moved on. Some of those Indians are still here."

"The Indians were saying Tah oka, Tah oka so we named our town Tahoka. I asked, "By chance is there a salty lake around here?"

"O Yes, it is North East of town" I was told by the town's people. I asked, "Do you happen to have a spring that feeds the lake?" "Yes, that is where we get our fresh water for our town," They replied.

Then I asked, "By chance is there anyone around that is Indian?"

"Oh yes, the Vo-tech teacher in the town to the south is an Indian. I think he said Choctaw or something like that. His family has been in the area a long time."

I went to that town, (O'Donnell, Tx, the same town that Hoss Cartright or Dan Blocker of the TV series Bonanza, grew up) and visited with the vo-tech teacher and his classes and shared this migration story. Of course he did not know anything about it except to say that his family has been here for a number of years. I gave out some books to him and he made a metal cross out of horseshoes.. And he was Choctaw.

I spent some time making an author visit to the Tahoka schools and the video of "Catch A Rabbit" on youtube.com was taken at the Tahoka school library. Just google youtube.com for Ralph Williston.

I looked up the words in the Choctaw dictionary for "Tah" and Oka and it means "bad water." This turned out to be a very interesting "possible connection" to this migration story. On another visit, I mentioned the research on the meaning of Tahoka, but the city fathers maintained that the word meant "fresh water" rather than "bad water." I decided that sometimes one cannot change history.

I visited with the Choctaw in Mississippi in the town of Philadelphia and asked if they still have the "pointing pole" and they always said, "it's in the cemetery.". I found out that they know where it is but their leaders want them to say, "It's in the cemetery, because they are preserving it."

Charlie Jones of the Mississippi Choctaw said that before they were forcibly moved, they "hugged the trees" to say goodbye before the soldiers drove them through mud and swamp land in the winter months many without shoes or blankets, to the present site near Talahina, Oklahoma. The capital of the Oklahoma Choctaw is south and west of Talahina called Tuskahoma.

A few things I recall when I was young.

I did not know that my father was a native Indian when I was growing up. He was just Dad. He taught music for 25 years and then Spanish for 10 more years. When I interviewed him he finally talked about his parents. The only thing he could remember was that his dad would come home late after playing his violin at some dance, and he played his violin as he came home over the pasture after being paid with alcohol. His dad died when he was very young.

As a child, Dad was placed in a boarding school which he ran away from, only to return years later to teach music at that same boarding school called Chilocco Indian School in north central Oklahoma. (I found a picture of the boarding school.)

He was forced to learn English. He was beaten if he talked his own language and ended up hopping on a railroad car and ended up at a Baptist high school near Muskogee, Oklahoma called Bacone.

While in high school, he remembered some people came to him and said, "You did not pay your back taxes on your land. But we will buy your land and pay your taxes for you. Thus he lost his land that his family had homesteaded to because he had not paid his back taxes that he did not owe. Fortunately, he used the money to go to Northeastern Teachers College, Tahlequah, Oklahoma, where he got his first degree.

His love of music kept him in high school and in college. On his first teaching job (as a 6th grade elementary teacher) he wanted to develop a music program. He was walking down a street called Choctaw in the town of Fairland, OK. He heard someone playing the trumpet. His name was Vern and was the brother of a young college girl, Mabel. They met and later married. (Vern later flew planes in WWII and through out his life).

Mabel, a white girl, (who we found out years later had native blood) played the piano and he played the violin. More of his story will come later.

Introduction to the "My White Dove" story

Little Eagle has learned to read the smoke signals from the various tribe around his village in case a scout is needed. He was surprised when the cliff village signaled that they were building a rope bridge and needed help. It was fall and they wanted to finish it before winter.

He asked grandfather about going. He knew that Grandfather would know about any need for scouts. Grandfather shook his head up and down and said, "We will expect you back after winter. It did not take long for Little Eagle to pack up his pony and head for the cliff village. He faintly remembered his experience taking a family up a cliff and every rock he stepped on broke and everyone was in trouble.

So, as he was riding, he recalled the one word, "Black," the Great Spirit had whispered in his mind. Then he found the strong black rocks to use as climbing rocks to get to the top of a high cliff. He'd rather not climb that cliff again so he headed around the cliff and valley. It took longer but he was not in a hurry.

As he approached the cliffs, and before he went around them and the river at the bottom, he looked up and felt his fear again when he and his first family as a scout was "trapped on that cliff." He went up stream and found a narrow place in the river and went across to the other side. He found a well-used trail that went up and stopped just outside the cliff village.

Their scout came and took him to their village grandmother. The scout said that their tradition was that any visitor must see the grandmother first. Little Eagle stood just outside the home of the grandmother and waited. While he waited, he studied their homes. The scout said their homes were made of logs and called "hogan."

The hogan was made of thick logs connected together at the ends into an eight-sided shape. Their homes had a smoke hole at the top and a door that had furry leather flaps that overlapped. The door faced east. Their scout said that Grandmother had the gift. As a scout, Little Eagle knew what that meant.

"Come In" said a young voice. Little Eagle pushed aside the thick leather door and ducked as he entered. When his eyes adjusted to the dim light of the small campfire, he could see a young girl sitting next to a wise looking grandmother. Both were facing the fire.

"Welcome to our village" the young girl said. "Grandmother wants to thank you for coming to help build a rope bridge across the cliff."

The young girl had a nice inviting voice. The grandmother still did not say anything. He waited and finally said, "My name is Little Eagle and I come from the prairie village." Little Eagle kept his sentence short and spoke clearly and carefully. The wise one motioned with her hand for him to sit next to her on a thick soft buffalo skin with fur.

She still did not say anything but had a nice smile. Little Eagle had learned that it was normal when meeting important people to wait a long time between their conversations. Meanwhile he studied this strange shaped home. It had a small campfire in the middle and the smoke would slowly lift and go out through the top. He could tell that it was a cooking fire since they did not need very much heat at this time of the year.

He noticed strange round green garden products (that he learned later were watermelons) circled the inside of the Hogan next to the wall. He learned later that during the winter the watermelons provided them with much needed water during the winter months when their spring was frozen over.

He knew both of them were silently studying him and searching for his spirit. He had known that this search was the gift that wise natives had because of their experience and age. He had already felt their spirit even when he was outside of the Hogan. He was taught to let that happen.

Grandmother finally said, "I want to thank you."
Little Eagle waited...

She repeated, "I want to thank you for bringing my family up the cliff."
Little Eagle searched his mind, trying to remember that family. The only thought he had was the fear he felt during that first

scout experience. He must have had a puzzled look on his face because she said,

"This is White Dove."

"When she was born my daughter looked out and the first thing she saw became the name for her baby girl."

Grandmother and her daughter saw a beautiful white dove flying overhead.

"The Great Spirit whispered to her and said that would be my granddaughter's name."

He knew not to interrupt. He wanted to say, "That is the tradition of my village too."

Grandmother hinted that he should know White Dove but he didn't. Both of them had such a good spirit that he was comfortable sitting inside their strange home. He waited for her next words.

But the young girl said, "Grandmother is tired now, but her spirit says that you are welcome to stay and help."

The young girl had such a nice voice and beautiful eyes.

 "You still don't remember me do you?" she said. Then I knew she had the gift too.

"I heard you ask the Great Spirit for help when we were trapped on that cliff."

He searched his memory again and wished he could remember. He remembered taking a family up a cliff and this young girl was not with the family.

"You still don't remember do you." She had read my mind and knew my thoughts. I knew she had the gift like her grandmother. She had the Great Spirit to help her know the thoughts of others.

In his mind he thought, "I still can't remember," even though he felt that fear that he had when every rock broke and he was hanging by his arms." He was a little uncomfortable knowing she knew what he was thinking. She continued.

"I was the one who was hanging onto your back and I felt you shaking. I knew that you had asked the Great Spirit for help."
Now he remembered that little girl. "Yes, I was the one." She said. "You have grown up." Little Eagle finally stuttered.
Illustration by Joan Shaw

He thought, "You probably knew what the Great Spirit had said."

"Yes." She nodded her head.

He had to change the subject. "When do we start on the rope bridge?" and they left the hogan.

"Tomorrow." She said in that soft pretty voice.

"I have never seen one." He thought.

"Someone goes to the other side and then our scout shoots an arrow with a leather string attached into a tree on the other side," she described.

"They attach a small rope to the string, then gradually larger and larger ropes until there are many ropes across the cliffs on each side." White Dove continued.

"Then you will climb out on the ropes and tie cross ropes and use two ropes to hang onto as you walk across."

He could not say anything as he tried to picture what it takes to build a rope bridge and finally asked, "How do you keep the wind from blowing and rocking the rope bridge?"

White Dove continued in that interesting voice, "Four ropes are attached to the middle on each side and two are tied to a rock or tree on each side so that four ropes keep it from rocking back and forth."

He became more comfortable with her.

"The women will bring food each day for you and the others. They have made ropes all summer out of buffalo, deer and bear skin" continued White Dove.

"Bears?" Little Eagle thought.

"Yes, we have bears here and wolves and mountain lions and coyotes and..." She responded.

"She did it again. She knew what I had said to myself. I was uncomfortable because I had interrupted her description of what the ropes were made of." Little Eagle thought.

Little Eagle slowly raised his hand which in his tradition meant that he was ready to go.

"Ok," she said. "I will take you where you will be staying. Go ahead and get your stuff off your pony and follow me."

There were a number of visitors setting up their teepees and he followed her to a large hogan which he felt must be her family's hogan. He met her mother and father and other younger children and family members. He thought, "Maybe the children would like to hear about some of my adventures."

"Yes, they would. I have told them about being trapped on the cliff many times and they would love to hear other stories," said White Dove having read Little Eagle's mind.

That night he went to his blanket very late because the children wanted to hear more and more stories. White Dove's mother let them stay up. We ate and ate and ate.

This is just the beginning of the story, "My White Dove."

"Run over by Buffalo" Introduction."

White Dove remembered that she had sat down with Grandfather and said, "I would like to be a scout like Little Eagle and I know that our native nation will let me be a scout. I think I can be a better scout than Little Eagle." Grandfather didn't say a word but days later he put his hand gently on her shoulder and she knew that she must come to his hogan just when the sun comes up the next morning.

She had had one journey and that was called "Snake Bit." She got up real early the next morning and waited until the door flap was opened. It was always opened briefly every morning (summer and winter) to greet the sun and to let the stale air out. Grandfather finally said, "For your next journey I want you to take a family into the prairie to their village. Sometime during this journey you will have a test. Ask our village scout if you can go and help take care of the children as you travel.

She did and Little Eagle said, "Sure."

The next day they packed up their ponies and left. As they were traveling, she thought about her first journey into a desert. Little Eagle drank water that had become poisoned and how she had tried everything to help him and finally she asked the Great Spirit for help.

The Great Spirit did help with three words...

While they were traveling through the woods and through the forest and into the tall prairie grass, she remembered asking Grandfather, "Why does the Great Spirit give me more words than Little Eagle? It surprised her when Grandfather said, "That is because you will have harder tests than Little Eagle."

She remembered saying to herself, "That's not fair." But she was willing to accept the challenge. She knew that if she stayed close to the Great Spirit that she would always have the same gift as her grandmother.

By sensing the needs of the children and family, she was welcomed to be a "part of the family" on the trip to the prairie village. She had never been to the prairie before so she was enjoying the trip. She also wondered what her next test would be.

Days went by and they were camped out in the tall prairie grass around a fire when she felt the ground shake. She ran to Little Eagle and whispered, "Why is the ground shaking?" He walked very fast (he did not want to alarm the children) up to the top of a little hill.

He saw hundreds of buffalo stampeding through the prairie grass. He ran down to White Dove and said, "There are hundreds of buffalo running right toward us and we cannot out run buffalo. We are going to get run over!"

White Dove thought, "This must be my test."

There were no trees or large rocks or anything to climb up on. Quickly she said in her mind, "O Great Spirit. We are all in trouble and need help."

White Dove listened and the Great Spirit only said one word, "Black."

"Black? How can that help us?" White Dove thought. The ground was now shaking harder and the sound of thousands of sharp hooves was getting louder and louder. The family was scared because they did not know what was making that loud rumble and why the ground was shaking under their feet. White Dove looked around to find anything that was black in color. The only thing that was black was a large black buffalo skin on one of the ponies that was used as a floor in a teepee.

White Dove yelled, "Grab that buffalo skin and all of us get under it." which they did. The buffalo came over the hill and now the family knew why the ground was shaking and what was making the sound. The children began to cry. White Dove tried to be calm and hummed to the children.

Guess what happened when the buffalo got to the buffalo skin?

The huge animals did not stop...they did not go around, but the buffalo jumped right over their large buffalo skin with everybody huddled underneath. Maybe they thought it was another buffalo, so they did not run over it.

When the buffalo had gone and everyone was out from under that buffalo skin, White Dove looked toward the direction that the buffalo had come, and said, "Why is there smoke over the hill?" Little Eagle ran up that little hill and saw a huge prairie fire. He thought "that fire must have been started by lightning and that is the reason the buffalo were stampeding."

For a strong wind was blowing the prairie fire and it had chased the buffalo right toward them. He ran to White Dove and said, "We are all in trouble again, there's a fire coming and we have nowhere to go and we cannot out run it."

She thought, "this must be another one of my tests," and quickly asked for help in her mind.

The Great Spirit this time said three words that she did want to do. "Start a Fire?" She did not understand. A fire is coming? But she obeyed and took burning sticks from their campfire and burned a big circle in the tall grass around them and said, "Pour all of our water on the buffalo skin in the middle of this circle and get under it."

The prairie fire came over the hill and it was getting hotter and hotter under that buffalo skin. Guess what happened when the fire got to the buffalo skin?

It didn't stop, it didn't go around, but the fire being blown by the strong wind, jumped right over them like the buffalo had jumped over the buffalo skin. They could feel the heat of the fire going over them.

Soon the prairie fire was gone and they crawled out from under the black buffalo skin and thanked the Great Spirit for telling White Dove what to do.

White Dove and Little Eagle took the family to their village and came back and shared their adventures with the village. White Dove realized that she had passed two more tests toward becoming a scout.

(Oops, I told the rest of this story, didn't I? I was supposed to stop somewhere in the middle.)

Introduction to "Caught in a Flash Flood"

On this journey, White Dove travels with Little Eagle into the mountains. They camp out at the foot of beautiful mountains and a valley. Grandfather had said that she would again have a test toward becoming a scout. During the night, White Dove is awakened by lightning and thunder from the tops of the mountains. She asked the Great Spirit what she should do and was told six words….

Then she went back to sleep. But they were awakened with the sounds of water rushing down the mountain called a flash flood. White Dove said…The Great Spirit told me…

Now you make up an ending for this story.

"White Dove, Catch Your Pony"

One of the most difficult journeys for White Dove was when grandfather had said, "White Dove, catch your pony." He had handed her a rope. "You can put this rope around your pony's neck, but you cannot tie it, your pony must become your friend."

White Dove had been watching the ponies near her village and had picked a beautiful white pony. But it was big and fast and wild. Day after day she studied the movements of all the ponies. When and where did they go to drink water, when and where did they graze, when and where did they separate and find shelter.

By the end of the summer months she did not have a plan on how she was going to even get close to her white pony. Or how she would separate it from the rest of the horses or how she could trap her pony from the rest of the horses in the blind valley where they drank spring water.

It was getting harder and harder for her pony to find good green grass and so it was now eating brown dried-up prairie scrub grass. She had gathered some nice green grass and piled it up in a basket but it had turned brown and some animal found it and ate it one night.

She thought about hiding some of the spring water in a cave so when the watering hole for the horses froze in the winter, she could offer her pony a drink. But she had no idea how to get close or even get her pony away from his family and come to her. She did ask her grandmother and she said, "Animals see pictures that are in your mind. You might want to go out and sit near the ponies and put a picture of green grass or juicy red apples or the cave shelter where there would be space for one pony to find shelter from the cold."

So day after day, she would sit near the ponies and put pictures of nice green grass, or big red apples or where the large cave was. She would close her eyes and sit quietly and sometimes she would hear one of the ponies slowly walk up to her and then it would run away.

Finally, she decided that she could not come up with any plan to catch her beautiful white pony, because it was "big" and could run really "fast." Since it had never been ridden and it was very "wild", she decided that she needed some help. So in her mind she said, "O Great Spirit, I am having trouble coming up with a plan on how I can catch my pony."

She listens and four words came to her. She could not think of how those four words would help her get close to her pony, much less help the pony become her friend or how she could help her pony to lose his "wildness." It must become tame enough for her to put the rope around his neck and a blanket over him, climb up on his back and use his neck mane to guide him and to ride him.

The four words were, "Wait till it rains." "It does not rain very much here." White Dove whispered to herself. "And how would that help me catch my white pony?"

But she decides to obey. She waits and waits and finally it rains and rains and rains. The valley where the horses live gets really muddy. It gets so muddy, that the horses who do not like mud, leave the muddy valley. But one pony cannot leave the valley because its hoofs are caught deep in the mud and the mud is halfway up his legs and he is now so tired from trying to jump up and from struggling to get out of the mud that he cannot hold up his head. His mouth and nose is filling with mud and he is getting weaker and weaker and is in "trouble."

White Dove sees "her pony" and now knows what to do. She gets some of the grass she has been collecting and fills her water bag with some water and she walks down into that deep mud. The mud comes up to her knees and then comes up to the top of her legs and then up to her waist. But she gets to her pony and pets her pony and feeds and waters her pony and her pony becomes "her friend."

While she is struggling to pull her pony's legs out of the mud, she discovers that she cannot pull her feet or legs out of the sticky mud. Now she and her pony are both trapped in the mud. The village is close enough to hear her screams, but she does not want to scare her pony. Besides it would be very embarrassing to admit that she was so foolish to walk down into that mud after her pony and it would hurt her pride.

White Dove decides to silently ask for some help. So in her mind she says. "O Great Spirit. We are both stuck in this mud and now we will both starve and die together. Please help us." She listens and she hears only two words. No way does she want to obey these two words! The two words did not make any sense.

She continues to think in her mind, "Why would I want to do what the Great Spirit wants me to do? Maybe I have heard the wrong two words?" But she has always trusted what the Great Spirit has whispered to her so she "laid down."

She lays down in that sticky, dirty mud. The mud comes up to her waist and up her arms and shoulders and neck and then up into her hair. Mud gets into her ears, but just when the mud gets up around her face…guess what? One of her legs pops out of the mud! Then the other leg popped out of the mud! And then both legs were free.

Now she knows what to do next. She whispers into one of her pony's ears, "Lay Down. Lay Down." Now, her pony does not want to lay down in that mud! No way does her pony want to lay down! White Dove gently pushes on her pony's neck and the mud goes up around his shoulders and then over his back. White Dove gently pushes on her pony and whispering in his ear, "Lay down, lay down."

Slowly her pony leans over and the mud comes up his neck and gets into his mane he doesn't like it so he shakes his head and throws mud into her face. But she continues to whispers into her pony, "lay down, lay down."

Her pony slowly leans over and the mud comes up to his head and into his ears. But when the mud is around his long nose and face, guess what? One of his legs pop out of the mud. Then another leg and another and finally all four legs are free and they both are free and both laying down in that mud.

She slowly "swims" out of the mud using her arms and legs and goes out of the mud. Her pony slowly rolls over on his back and lays in that mud. White Dove now rolls him over his back again and again until they are both out of that muddy valley and standing together.

Her pony lets her slowly put the rope around its neck and she remembers Grandfather's instructions. "Now you can put this rope around your pony's neck, but do not tie it. Your pony must become your friend." And they both walk out of that valley and she is so happy that she has passed two tests toward becoming a scout.

They reach the village and grandfather meets her and her pony and reaches out to touch her shoulder like he always does when she has trusted the Great Spirit and says, "White Dove. Go to the river and wash!"

She had forgotten that they were both covered with mud. So they went together to the village lake and she washed and washed all of the mud from her feet and legs and arms, stomach and out of her ears and the mud out of her hair. And then she washed the mud from her pony's hoofs and legs and back and stomach and from his neck and his mane and his ears and from around his long nose and face.

She put the rope over her pony's neck and did not tie it. She put her arms around her pony's neck and gently grabbed his mane with her hands and slowly climbed onto his back. She held onto his mane and the loose rope to keep from sliding off his back. She rode her pony for the first time back to the village. She "tied" the pony outside her hogan by draping the rope over a bush and gave him grass to eat and water to drink.

At the village fire, Grandfather gently placed his hand on her shoulder and said, "We watched you sit in the field for days. We watched you get drenched by the rain.

Then we watched you walk down into that mud carrying grass and water. We watched you feed and water your pony and we watched you pet your pony. But we did not understand why you would want to lay down in that deep mud."

Grandfather finally said, "White Dove you have passed two more tests toward becoming a scout. Look what the village family have prepared for you and your pony. ...all kinds of food...

And there was another blanket. The village people had filled another blanket with all shapes and colors and sizes of beads! They knew that one of the most favorite things you did was to make rings, necklaces, bracelets out of beads for the village people. So White Dove ate some food and started to make rings, necklaces, bracelets out beads by stringing the beads through tiny strips of dried leather strings called "sinew." She used long cactus needles attached to the sinew to string the beads.

That night as she was warming up and drying out her clothes, she told about how the Great Spirit had told her four words first and then two words. She told how her beautiful white pony, even though he was big and fast and wild became her friend. That night she dreamed of passing the rest of her tests toward leading others through the woods and forests and deserts and mountains. She thanked the Great Spirit for helping her pass two tests in one long journey that took all summer.

She also thought, "I know that I can be a better scout than the guys because I will have harder tests than the guys.

Author note:
> During my studies with the natives I discovered that one way they "tamed" the wild horses was to drive them into a pond or lake or muddy area. They would then slowly climb onto them and "ride them" as they would buck until their horse was so tired, it would stop bucking, and walk, and then stop moving completely. This method was not so hard on the horse or the rider as compared to the common image of the rodeo "bucking bronco" method of breaking down wild horses.

Summary of future stories cont.

After being "wrapped in a marriage blanket," White Dove and Little Eagle are caught in a dense fog at night and now must find their way out of the forest and back to their village.

In another journey, she and Little Eagle are caught in a snow storm. They had found protection from the cold in the same cave that Little Eagle had found when he was attacked by wolves. They had kept warm and had water and now running out of wood for the fire and are now starving. Little Eagle had left when the storm had let up to go back to the village for food. White Dove had stayed to watch over the ponies. Then the snow storm started up again and the wind is stronger and colder. He had not come back. The sun is going down and the snow drifts are now covering up the cave entrance. White Dove stood at the entrance to keep the light of the fire as bright as possible. Over and over she calls out his name. It is getting darker and darker, colder and colder and now she is worried.

You will have to wait for these and other stories that will come out sometime.

End Notes by the author:

Our life now is filled with traveling to schools, teaching writing workshops, making author visits to libraries, homes and churches. I am developing walking and riding trails and fly my drone that I call the eagle, driving the tractor and riding in parades with our six wheeler (Argo) that I call "the buffalo," taking astronomy pictures through the telescope and working on inventions. I dream of developing our acreage into a gathering place with a primitive camp and story telling campfire site that we can invite folks and children to come and hear these ageless stories as long as I am able. I do have a demo story "Catch A Rabbit" on youtube.com. Just go to youtube.com and type in Ralph Williston.

Our children still want me to get the other stories into books. I am considering producing a "thumb drive" or SD card filled with videos of sharing stories with the children over the years.

Every story has many gestures.

When asked by a child, "How old are you." I always say..."Old enough to be your grandfather." Natives believe that trees talk and that you can talk to them and they will talk to you. So that tree behind me is saying, you can last as long as me."

I was supposed to put the above picture of my full blood Choctaw father in the "Corn Seed Test" story book and forgot. "Get your corn to grow as tall as Grandfather's corn plant."

Dad taught music for 25 years and Spanish for 10 more years. In high school he was known as "the music man" because he could play every instrument. I remember when I was in high school that I had to learn to play whatever instrument he needed in the band. And he made his own instruments even a Viola and a "bottle band" made out of bottles filled with various levels of water to produce sounds of eight octaves and it took four people to play all of them. Dad taught me as a teenager how to tune and repair pianos and I still have some of his tools. Sometimes we do not really appreciate a person until too late.

30 sticks & Light Horsemen

While visiting the Choctaw museum at the Choctaw capital building in Tuskahoma, Oklahoma, I saw an exhibit that showed a blue uniform with the name tag, "Williston, Light Horseman."

After tracking down my favorite Choctaw storyteller and humble historian, "Charlie Jones." I asked him about this part of the Choctaw history. This is roughly what he shared:

"There was a time after following the "pointing pole" and migrating from the southwest and naming the wide river "Mississippi" and the "Choctaw trail of tears and arrival to "Indian territory" now called by a Choctaw name "Okla" meaning man and "homa" meaning red."

(I had learned that one does not get in a hurry when you talked to Charlie, but to just sit back, and listen, and try to be patient, and wait until he gets to your question.)

Charlie Jones then continued.

"After kissing the trees goodbye in the homeland north of Jackson, near a town called today as Philadelphia, in the state of Mississippi, and carrying the bones of our families, walking to this new land, we made this new land our home."

"White men became our friends and they had laws to be obeyed and when one of the Choctaw broke a law, the law men could not find the Choctaw. These lawmen knew that the Choctaw could find other Choctaw and they came to a young Choctaw and gave him a title..."light horseman." The lawmen would give the young man 30 sticks. The light horseman would go and find the "wanted" person and give them the 30 sticks. And tell them to throw away one stick each day and when they were gone, they must come to town. Respect and honor and honesty was the fabric of the Choctaw and so the wanted person would come to town and turn themselves into the lawmen."

Now I know that a Williston was a piece of that Choctaw History. Today one of the councilmen for the Choctaw nation is a relative called Thomas Williston.

Dad told me when he was a young child that a grandmother saved his life. He remembered that he was at a church meeting when some white men came through the church doors riding their horses and shooting their guns. He remembered that when a gun was pointed toward him, a grandmother hit the shotgun upward just before it went off and that it made a big hole in the church roof. She saved him from being shot.

When I sit down with the children I always say, "You can be in my next book. I need artists to illustrate my stories. I have trouble drawing "stick people!"   Send me a drawing and send it by e-mail to nancy.k.williston@gmail.com.

Here is a drawing made by one of my listeners called nannynonna who sent this drawing and I do not have her current e-mail. I wish I could find her and give her this book.

When I sit down with children I would also say, "Now, do you know what e-mail stands for according to Ralph?" "e-mail stands for, "eagle mail" because it flies from your computer from tower to tower and lands on my computer.

Practice your drawing and painting of pictures because your pictures could be in a future book and you can keep track of future books by going to www.little-eagle.com.